ACOUSTIC**R&B**FOR **MODERN**GUITAR

Learn Fresh R&B Acoustic Guitar Chord Voicings, Licks, Fills, Grooves & Tunes

SIMON**PRATT**

FUNDAMENTAL**CHANGES**

Acoustic R&B for Modern Guitar

Learn Contemporary R&B Chord Voicings, Licks, Fills, Grooves & Performance Pieces

Published by **www.fundamental-changes.com**

ISBN: 978-1-78933-405-0

Copyright © 2023 Simon Pratt

Edited by Joseph Alexander & Tim Pettingale

www.fundamental-changes.com

Over 11,000 fans on Facebook: **FundamentalChangesInGuitar**

Instagram: **FundamentalChanges**

For over 350 Free Guitar Lessons with Videos Check Out

www.fundamental-changes.com

Cover Image Copyright: Shutterstock, Africa Studio

Music Contributed by Kerry "2 Smooth" Marshall

Contents

Introduction

Welcome to *Acoustic R&B for Modern Guitar*!

The roots of rhythm and blues (R&B) are found in gospel, soul, Motown, funk, pop and jazz, and the guitar has always been a key instrument in this music, often creating the backbone for classic tracks via a catchy hook or funky rhythmic groove.

Over the years, R&B has been on an epic journey…

Throughout the late 1950s into the '60s, Detroit was a major hub for R&B and soul artists. It became known as the "Motor City" because of its connection to the car manufacturing industry, and this was often shortened to "Mo Town" – which eventually gave its name to the iconic record label. Despite being just one record label, Motown quickly came to describe an entire genre of music.

Motown's house band of session musicians were known as The Funk Brothers and played on some the biggest hits of this era. The band's nucleus consisted of iconic musicians such as Benny "Papa Zita" Benjamin on drums and James Jamerson on bass, and they were joined by a host of incredible musicians who made up their personnel over the years.

Motown was one of the first forms of pop music to transcend race and soon became known as the "sound of young America". Acts such as The Marvellettes, The Four Tops, The Supremes, Marvin Gaye, and Stevie Wonder help to evolve the sound. The other major hub producing R&B was Memphis, which introduced acts such as Otis Reading, Steve Cropper and Booker T and The M.G.'s, Bill Withers and Aretha Franklin.

There are too many great guitar players from this era to mention them all here, but throughout the early period of R&B, influential players included Melvin M. Ragin (aka "Wah Wah Watson" of The Funk Brothers), Cornell Dupree, Cornelius Grant (The Temptations), Steve Cropper, and Curtis Mayfield, to name a few.

Fast forward a couple of decades and we have the emergence of Neo Soul – an important hybrid form of R&B. The term "Neo Soul" is not a new one, it was first coined by producer Kedar Massenburg (president of Motown Records from 1997-2004) when he needed a phrase to describe a genre that embraced the influence of modern electronic musical styles but also acknowledged earlier forms of soul music.

At the time, Massenburg had signed breakthrough artist Erykah Badu, who somewhat defied categorization. Along with other critical artists of the early 90s, such as D'Angelo, Lauren Hill and Maxwell, the foundations of Neo-Soul were laid, and the success of D'Angelo's 1995 album *Brown Sugar* was pivotal in bringing the sound of Neo-Soul to the masses.

Neo-Soul suffered a decline in the mid-to-late 2000s, but since 2010 onwards has enjoyed a massive revival through artists such as Jill Scott, John Legend, Amy Winehouse, Leela James, Raheem DeVaughn and Mayer Hawthorne, to name just a few. During this resurgence, the acoustic guitar played a vital role in shaping the sound.

The guitar has continued to play an essential role in this music, and this has ushered in a new generation of R&B-influenced guitar players. Social media has played its part too, with platforms like Instagram bringing wide acclaim to guitar players such as Mateus Asato, Todd Pritchard and Kerry "2Smooth" Marshall. Then, players such as Isaiah Sharkey, Mark Lettieri, and many more are carrying the torch for this music into the future.

In this book, you'll learn the techniques and concepts of R&B guitar, old school and modern. You'll build your musical vocabulary by learning R&B-orientated chord voicings, triad ideas, and lots of cool licks and fills. You'll also learn how to create R&B guitar parts from scratch, play full arrangements of original acoustic R&B tunes, and learn useful chord progressions you can use in your own songwriting.

I've also included a Spotify playlist of tracks you should know, so before you play a note, kick back with your favourite headphones and spend some time familiarising yourself with the sound of this great music. You can check out the playlist here:

https://geni.us/aRnBspotify

If you are new to this style, I recommend working through the book from start to finish. Take your time to work through each section and make sure you feel comfortable with the material in each chapter before you move on. If you are more experienced, feel free to dive in wherever you like.

These examples will work equally well on an acoustic or electric guitar, but the audio examples were recorded on my Taylor acoustic.

Happy Playing!

Simon

Get the Audio and Video

The audio files for this book are available to download for free from **www.fundamental-changes.com.** The link is in the top right-hand corner. Click on the "Guitar" link then simply select this book title from the drop-down menu.

We recommend that you download the files directly to your computer, not to your tablet, and extract them there before adding them to your media library. You can then put them onto your tablet, iPod or burn them to CD. On the download page there are instructions, and we also provide technical support via the contact form.

For over 350 free guitar lessons with videos check out:

www.fundamental-changes.com

Join our free Facebook Community of Cool Musicians

www.facebook.com/groups/fundamentalguitar

Tag us for a share on Instagram: **FundamentalChanges**

Get the Video

We had a lot of fun recording videos for each of the longer pieces in this book. You can access them here:

https://www.fundamental-changes.com/acousticrbvideos/

https://geni.us/acou

Or scan this QR code:

Chapter One – Chord Progressions

Chord sequences on guitar have an integral function in R&B and often act as the main hook of the song. Because R&B is a fusion of so many other genres (including soul, gospel, funk and jazz), the choice of chords available for us to draw from is enormous.

This chapter is all about the foundational chord sequences commonly heard in R&B, all voiced to sound great on acoustic guitar.

This chapter is divided into sections, based on the number of chords in a sequence. In contrast to other styles of music, many R&B tracks are built on a hook of just two chords. Remember this when you are creating your own songs, or when you're jamming. Often, fewer chords played with an interesting approach will get you a lot further than a complicated sequence.

The ideas here are generally built around a simple "core" progression, for example F Major to C Major. But then I'll show you the R&B-style voicings I use to add extra elements to the basic chords. For example, the sequence might say F Major, but I might play FMaj7 or Fsus2. Or, I might add a fill that includes extended chord tones in order to freshen up the harmony and capture the listener's attention.

The most important thing to keep in mind when playing this music is that it's all about the *vibe*. It's much more about *how* rather than *what* we play. Even when playing just two chords, we can inject emotion and a *feel* into the music that causes people to respond and groove along with us.

In the examples that follow, when you hear an idea or riff you really like, work with it, loop it around and develop it to make it your own.

Let's get started.

Two-Chord Progressions

We start with the aforementioned chord sequence based on the movement from F to C. It's a popular chord sequence seen in all types of music, from pop-rock to choral sequences. Here, it's freshened up with an Fsus2 voicing.

The strumming pattern is loose, and the voicings use the middle strings in order to highlight the resolution of Fsus2 to F to C.

Example 1a

When I think about playing any chord sequence, I always have in mind a strummed pattern and a single note picked pattern, so that I've got different textures to use over a track. For example, we could use a strumming pattern for the chorus and a picking pattern for the verse. This example shows a picking pattern you could use to articulate the sequence in Example 1a. You can fingerpick, pick or even hybrid-pick (pick and fingers) this idea, the choice is yours.

Example 1b

Alternating between a bass note and other fragments of a chord is an important technique for creating R&B-type grooves from simple to complex. Example 1c shows a common movement between GMaj7 and AMaj7 (you can easily move these barre chords to any key).

Example 1c

The next popular sequence is F to Am7. You've probably played it hundreds of times, but the addition of some simple embellishments help to turn it into something much more interesting. Here I used muted strummed notes to add a percussive element and single line fills at the end of each bar, using the notes of the A Natural Minor scale.

Example 1d

Example 1e uses the sequence of Dm to G. Instead of regular open chords, I've used some fun voicings to give it an old-school gospel flavour.

Example 1e

Minor chords are important in acoustic R&B, since so many tunes use them. The next example shows a sequence of Am7 – Dm7 that uses open voicings. The single string notes help to glue the chords together and give the line some movement.

Example 1f

Example 1g shows the same sequence played with barre chords. The fills are built from the A Minor Pentatonic and A Natural Minor scales.

You'll probably hear a nod to Jimi Hendrix's *Little Wing* in this idea. Though known for his rock years, Hendrix began his career as a sideman for soul and R&B musicians including Wilson Pickett, Sam Cooke, Jackie Wilson and Ike and Tina Turner – so the R&B vocabulary was always a part of his musical DNA.

Example 1g

Jumping forward in time, this idea is based on Montell Jordan's mid-1990s hit *This Is How We Do It,* based on a groove of Am to Bb.

Example 1h

Three-Chord Progressions

The previous section showed that something as simple as a two-chord progression is more than enough to build a great tune around, but now we move on to some three-chord ideas.

Example 1i demonstrates an Am – F – G sequence that uses ringing open chords. What I love most about this is the continuity between the chords created by maintaining the C note in all three voicings. The strategy of keeping one common note and arranging chord voicings around it is extremely effective, and it immediately adds a beautiful cohesion to any guitar part.

Example 1i

The next sequence is GMaj7 – Bm – A. At the end of bar two, the melodic fill uses the notes of the B Natural Minor scale. With a line like this, it's important to keep the note separation clean and clipped, because this is a big part of the modern R&B style. (Check out the tunes of India Arie for some beautiful examples).

This means that picking accuracy is paramount, and you'll also need to apply good picking hand muting to prevent the strings from ringing into each other.

Example 1j

Dm – G – C is a common sequence in modern R&B. The double-stop (two notes played together) licks in this example are built from the D Natural Minor scale.

Example 1k

This example is built around the sequence Em7 – A7 – Dmaj7. I wanted to use beautiful ringing open chords to accentuate the acoustic guitar tone and add depth to the music. These are some of my favourite chords and I recommend you commit this one to memory. The pull-off in the Dmaj7 chord is a nice way to continue the ringing sound.

Example 1l

When I first heard the song *State of Mind* by Raúl Midón, I was blown away by its beauty. When I figured out it used predominantly just three chords (Em7 – Bm7 – Am7) I was stunned. My version here doesn't include the harmonics he uses, but this example gives a flavour of this versatile sequence.

Example 1m

Four-Chord Progressions

Next, we move on to four-chord sequences. One of the most important chord sequences in music is the I vi IV V progression, which in the key of C Major is C – Am – F – G. This sequence appears everywhere in popular music (not just in R&B). Example 1n shows one way you can add an acoustic R&B flavour to this progression.

The C and Am chords include a simple picked pattern that's followed by a series of double-stops to create a call and response phrase. The three-note FMaj7 voicing is popular in modern Neo-Soul circles and a useful shape to know.

In gospel music, a suspended chord is often used to build tension before a strong resolution. Use suspended chords sparingly to add interest and an unexpected twist to your music. Here, I play the Gsus4 right at the end of bar three.

Example 1n

You never know when the inspiration and opportunity to transcribe something will grab you. When I was 12, I watched a show called *Fame Academy* where I heard the song *I Can't Break Down* by Sinead Quinn. I spent about a week figuring out the arpeggiated chord pattern at the start of the song. Doing this taught me the importance of transcription and also how difficult hearing open chords can be. Example 1o is my homage to a much younger me.

This sequence of Am – Em – F – Dm can be alternated picked, fingerpicked or hybrid-picked. Try all three to see which you prefer.

Example 1o

Just the Two Of Us by Bill Withers is one of the most iconic R&B tracks of all time. This A – G#7 – C#m7 – F#7 sequence teaches you how tracks like that can be built.

Example 1p

Example 1q demonstrates the sequence Dm – Am – Bb – Gm.

First practice playing the arpeggiated chords and learn the fills separately before combining them. I play this example quite loosely, so listen to the audio to capture the right feel.

Example 1q

The final sequence is based on *Happy* by Pharell Williams. Although I know the song well, I had never taken the time to transcribe it until now. I was pleasantly surprised when I did though, as I knew there was something about it that made my ears tingle. It features the chord sequence of Dbmaj7 – Cm7 – Cm7 – F. It's the repeating chord in the middle that is quite unusual. Check out *Hey Ya* by Outkast for more of the same.

Pay attention to the phrasing of the chords, as there's a lot of syncopation here.

Example 1r

For your reference, here are all the chord sequences featured in this chapter. I've included the key and each chord's Roman numeral position in the scale, so you can transpose them easily. Remember, you can always use a capo to play these ideas in other keys – even the ones with open strings.

Chord Sequence	Key	Roman Numerals
F – C	C	IV – I
GMaj7 – AMaj7	G	I – II (major)
F – Am7	Am	VI – i
Dm – G	C	ii – V
Am7 – Dm7 open chords	Am	i – iv
Am7 – Dm7 Barre	Am	i – iv
Am – Bb	Am	i – bII (minor)
Am – F – G	Am	i – VI – VII
GMaj7 – Bm – A	Bm	I – iii – II (major)
Dm – G – C	C	ii – V – I
Em7 – A7 – Dmaj7	D	ii – V – I
Em7 – Bm7 – Am7	Em	i – v – iv
C – Am – F – G	C	I – vi – IV – V
Am – Em – F – Dm	Am	i – v – VI –iv
A – G#7 – C#m7 – F#7	C#m	VI – V7 – i – IV7
Dm – Am – Bb – Gm	Dm	i – v – VI – iv
Dbmaj7 – Cm7 – Cm7 – F	F	bVI – vm – vm – I

Chapter Two – Chords, Fills, and Licks

In this chapter we'll work through a series of examples that take things a step further by teaching how to blend R&B chord voicings with licks and fills. Here you'll learn how to decorate and embellish chord voicings to create more interesting and melodic guitar parts for modern R&B.

Before we begin, I recommend listening to these following tracks to get into the vibe of this chapter. Although they are not strictly R&B tunes, they show how this style of playing has a broad application across musical genres.

- Mark Lettieri – *Montreal*

- Jimi Hendrix – *Little Wing*

- Stevie Ray Vaughan – *Lenny*

- George Benson – *Affirmation*

These combinations of jazz chords with beautiful fills shows what's possible when you master this style.

Let's begin by decorating some Major 7 chords.

One of the most common chord shapes in R&B is a Maj7 voicing with a root note on the low E string. This idea combines that voicing with G Major Pentatonic scale fills. It centres around double-stops and is reminiscent of Jimi Hendrix's approach in *Little Wing*.

Example 2a

Example 2b is another G Major scale idea. Gradually move this lick up the fretboard, one fret at a time, to see how it feels to play it in different positions.

Example 2b

In modern R&B guitar parts, it's common to hear a bar of single notes followed by a bar of double-stops (or vice versa). This example shows one of my favourite approaches to this technique and is again built around the GMaj7 voicing.

Example 2c

Let's move on and look at some ideas you can use to decorate minor chord voicings.

This Am7 chord is followed by a useful A Natural Minor phrase.

Example 2d

Now check out the following example. Listen to the audio and note how the sound differs to the previous idea.

Example 2e

What's different about Example 2e is that it uses the A Minor Pentatonic scale with an added note. Great players like Carlos Santana pioneered the use of the minor pentatonic with an added 9th, to convert the pentatonic into a hexatonic (six note) scale that sounds more sophisticated.

If you've never tried this idea before it's worth experimenting with. Below is a fretboard map showing A Minor Pentatonic with an added 9th (A B C D E G). Make yourself an Am chord vamp and use the map to jam over it and create some licks.

This lick uses the A Blues scale and combines legato and slides to create a smooth, free-flowing lick. Learn the chord shape first, then play the lick. This will help to connect the two ideas in your mind.

Example 2f

The next example shows an idea you can use on a dominant 7 chord.

Example 2g shows a funky A7 pattern reminiscent of *Cut the Cake* by Average White Band. This lick is heavily syncopated, so I recommend you listen to the audio a few times to hear how I play it. When you've learnt it, jam along with me to nail the phrasing.

Example 2g

A Dominant 7#5 chord is often used to create tension and a slight dissonance in R&B. This lick uses the A Altered scale and is in the style of the fantastic Chris Payton, an R&B, gospel, quartet, and Neo-Soul session master.

Example 2h

Let's return to Major 7th chords, but now look at decorations you can add to fifth string voicings.

We'll begin with this CMaj7 chord voicing, combined with a major pentatonic lick – a common sound in both R&B and Neo-Soul.

Example 2i

Building on the previous example, this example includes two voicings of CMaj7 and adds a chromatic rundown onto the end of a pentatonic lick.

Example 2j

Here are some fun sliding double-stop patterns around the C Major scale.

Example 2k

Let's look at some fifth string minor 7 chord ideas.

First is a lick based around Dm7 that uses the D Natural Minor scale. Experiment with alternate picking but if that's a challenge just use down strokes on the double-stops. Alternate picking is a great way to go with this kind of idea, but it can feel more difficult at first.

Example 2l

This lick is an absolute staple of my playing and I recommend you commit it to memory. It centres around the Dm7 chord and uses D Natural Minor scale to create the fill. It's a long line, so break it up and learn it one string at a time.

Example 2m

Here's a funky E Mixolydian line based around a James Brown style E9 chord. Check out *Papa's Got A Brand New Bag Pt 1* to hear this type of approach in action.

Example 2n

Now we have learned some important chord voicings and seen how to build R&B licks around them, it's time to combine them into longer, more musical sequences.

Example 2o uses the progression G – Bm – Em – C, and combines ideas you learned earlier in the chapter. You can hear how they connect together to create a cohesive guitar part.

Example 2o

Example 2p uses a Bm7 – GMaj7 – F#7 progression and adds B Natural Minor fills. It focuses heavily on double-stops and slides to create a signature modern R&B sound.

Example 2p

You may have noticed throughout this chapter that, more often than not, my modern R&B ideas are and built from four foundations:

- Start from a chord sequence

- Start from a lick or a hook

- Start from a melody

- Start from a rhythm / groove

To end this chapter, my challenge to you is to try and compose different ideas from each of these starting points.

These foundations will help you to write ideas that sound different, because the underlying focus will change. Every time you feel stuck, pick a different starting point from the list.

You can get going by varying the ideas in this chapter to make your own phrases. Think about altering the notes, the timing, the order of the chords, or even the time signature to create an original slant.

However, the next two chapters will teach you many more ideas to help create your own R&B guitar parts!

Chapter Three – How to Build R&B Guitar Parts (1)

Now that you've had a taste of the potential of modern R&B guitar for creating fresh musical ideas, let's take a step back and consider how to go about composing these ideas from scratch. What can we do when faced with a lead sheet that just has chord names on it?

In this chapter I'm going to teach you how to build tight, effective R&B guitar parts and explain approaches you can take with both rhythmic work and lead concepts.

All these examples are written to function in a full band setting. My aim is to show you how I approach writing, to equip you to create your own awesome R&B guitar parts that groove *hard*. We'll cover chord voicings, scale choices, fills, and there is even a full solo for you to learn.

Before you dive into the material, have a listen to Justin Timberlake's *Cry Me A River* for reference. Even though this tune is primarily keyboard based, the ideas played work equally well on guitar. The examples in this chapter use a similar chord progression.

That tune's R&B aesthetic, with a strong beat and a repetitive chord pattern, form the backbone of the track and make it a modern classic. The lesson here is, don't just listen to guitar parts for inspiration. Keyboards are a fundamental part of R&B, so don't be afraid to steal those ideas. Also, pay careful attention to the bass as it will teach you how to form strong rhythmic grooves.

The next two chapters are probably the most important for your development as a modern R&B player, so don't be afraid to camp out here and dig deep into the concepts. Try to write a few of your own variations for each idea – it's a great song writing exercise.

Rhythm Parts

When thinking about creating parts, you need to get deep into the chord sequence that underlies the song. Going deep is essential, as often R&B tunes revolve around a repetitive sequence, and this allows great freedom and the potential for development in the guitar part. The more you explore the possibilities, the more ideas you will come up with for interesting parts.

We are going to use the same chord sequence for the entire chapter to explore different ways of generating ideas.

NB: If the D#/G chord feels tricky, try leaving out the note on the 1st fret and just pluck the other three notes.

Example 3a

Playing each chord shape as an arpeggio is a solid beginning and easily creates a classic R&B vibe. You'll notice I add a rest between each chord which introduces space in the rhythm part. You'll hear this approach in a lot of tracks in this genre. More often than not, it's what you *don't* play that creates the groove!

Example 3b

Now let's add a rhythmic slap on beats 2 and 4 to create a more percussive rhythmic part. Do this by gently tapping the strings with the knuckles of you picking hand. You don't need to move your hand much, so you can continue fingerpicking immediately after the slap.

Example 3c

Example 3d shows a strumming pattern used in many modern R&B tracks.

If you find that your upstrokes are a bit clunky, try hitting just the top three strings. This will teach you the movement, then as you become more confident you will be able to add more strings to your upstroke. Check out the audio to get the groove.

Example 3d

Adding different voicings will make your guitar part sound quite different. Here, I introduce two important voicings for your R&B repertoire: the Minor 11 and Diminished chord shapes. Memorize them now, so you won't need to refer back here when you're jamming later.

Example 3e

Next, let's move on with a couple of examples that arpeggiate these chords, but not with the straight ascending pattern we used earlier. Here's a more intricate pattern that is very effective.

I've included fingerpicking instructions in the notation to show how I play the next example, using the classical Spanish naming method:

P = thumb

I = index

M = middle

A = ring

If this approach is new to you, practice the fingerpicking pattern in isolation before adding the chord changes. Pay attention to placement of the rests.

Example 3f

The rests leave us space to add fills between the chords. The slides in bar one uses the G# Minor Pentatonic scale. The sliding diminished chord shapes in bar two are a common R&B texture.

Example 3g

R&B guitar parts are often all about laying down a solid foundation on which the other instruments can build, especially the vocals. Sometimes fingerpicking alone is not quite enough to achieve this, so on those occasions I will use a syncopated strumming pattern like the one here.

Example 3h

Lead Parts

Let's move on and look at some typical lead parts and fills that work with our chord progression. Think of these ideas as "adding the secret sauce". As funny as that sounds, it's an important thing to remember because guitarists are often guilty of over-playing their parts. Tread lightly, leave space, and don't overdo the fills!

Before we get into the melodic ideas, let me spell out some useful scale patterns used in some of the examples. You're no doubt familiar with the Blues scale, but perhaps not used to playing it in G#.

Example 3i shows you the G# Blues scale played from its root note on the sixth string, 4th fret. It's the perfect sound to add fills to a G# minor chord sequence.

Example 3i

Now practice the G# Blues scale with its root on the fifth string.

Example 3j

This first example uses a lead technique called *staccato legato*. The idea is to play a hammer-on or pull-off *without* sustaining the note. In other words, once you have hammered on, quickly release the pressure with your finger while touching the string to stop the note. This is a modern R&B sound and is used by guitarists like Kerry "2 Smooth" Marshall. Example 3k illustrates this idea with the G# Blues scale.

Example 3k

Any performance can be ruined by either poorly executed, or non-appropriate vibrato. Although applying modern vibrato technique on an acoustic guitar is not common, it can be highly effective when used sparingly.

Slide the fretting finger above the fret then quickly return to pitch. Repeat this movement quickly to create a heavy vibrato.

Example 3l

Next is a G# Natural Minor scale fill that uses back-to-back slides to create a free-flowing lick. The fun thing is that it is played using slides on three different fingers in just one bar. The first slide pattern uses the second finger, the second pattern uses the third, and the final one uses the first.

Example 3m

Being able to voice a lick in a higher octave is very useful when you need to cut through a mix. Here's the previous example transposed up an octave. Make a point of learning all your phrases up an octave on a higher string set where possible.

Example 3n

I often use variations of this G# Natural Minor lick as an introduction before laying down a main groove. Play the first note with your second finger and the rest of the lick will fall under your fingers.

Example 3o

Combining Rhythm and Fills

Now that you have some rhythm parts and lead lines for this progression under your fingers, it's time to combine them.

This idea brings together the lick from the previous example with a fingerpicked version of our workhorse chord sequence.

Example 3p

If we combine the G#m7 sliding fill with a fingerpicked rhythm pattern it works well as an introduction idea. Try combining the ideas in this chapter freely and see what ideas those combinations evoke in your song writing.

Example 3q

To end this chapter, we have a full solo that brings together variations of the ideas we've covered. I wrote it specially to help you work on your soloing skills.

You can watch a video of me playing this piece via the links below. Use the backing track provided in the audio download to practice this over – and indeed, any of the soloing ideas we've discussed.

https://www.fundamental-changes.com/acousticrbvideos/

https://geni.us/acou

Example 3r – full solo

G#m7 C#m7 Emaj7 D#7#9 D#/G

G#m7 C#m7 Emaj7 D#7#9 D#/G

G#m7 C#m7 Emaj7 D#7#9 D#/G G#m7

Well done on completing this chapter. I believe it will be one you'll return to often. Record yourself playing everything you've learned, as this is a great way to document your progress and notice any areas that need improvement.

Chapter Four – How to Build R&B Guitar Parts (2)

In this chapter we'll use a similar process to the previous chapter to create some tight, effective R&B guitar parts over a new chord progression. The chord sequence and vibe here is inspired by Grover Washington's tune *Just the Two of Us*, featuring Bill Withers on vocals – an absolute R&B/soul masterpiece. If you've never heard it, check it out before diving into the examples.

Rhythm Parts

This time around, the major focus of the rhythm ideas will be how to use simple triads (three-note chords) to create some tight guitar parts.

While using barre chords is a valid and common approach to rhythm playing, you will often find that the keyboards or other instruments are fighting for the same sonic "real estate" in a track. Higher voiced triads that use smaller fragments of chord shapes will help to leave space for the bassist and other instruments, while still outlining the harmony.

My goal here is to open your eyes to the wonderful possibilities of triad shapes. They will not only change the way you approach rhythm playing but also open up new ideas for soloing strategies later – especially when playing more complex sequences.

Example 4a shows our next set of workhorse chords: Bmaj7 – A#7#5 – D#m9 – D#m9. The sequence is played with barre chords to begin with, just to get the sound of the progression in your head. In the next few examples I'll show you how to create triad patterns that outline this sequence.

Example 4a

First, let's isolate each chord and learn its triad *inversions* on the top four strings (i.e. all the same notes in a different order). Let's begin with the B Major triads.

Example 4b

Next, we will add fills to each of the middle string triad patterns. Learning to visualise a triad shape and the available embellishment notes around it is an integral part of playing R&B chord and lead parts.

Example 4c

Now let's learn some fills around the top string B Major triad shapes.

Example 4d

Example 4e shows the A#7 triad voicings on the same string sets as before.

Example 4e

There are many different scale choices that can be used to create fills over a dominant 7 chord, but here I'll be using the A# Mixolydian scale and the A# Altered scale.

Normally, the most interesting fills in modern R&B guitar tracks are played on dominant 7 chords, as they can handle more tension. Using the Mixolydian scale creates a traditional jazz/blues feel, while the altered scale sounds much more dissonant and "out there". You'll quickly hear which of the following lines are A# Mixolydian and which are A# Altered.

Here are some ideas for the middle string triads.

Example 4f

In Example 4g, I have outlined some fills based around the top string A#7 shapes. Altered scale ideas like these have a more exotic sound, so use them sparingly whenever you need to add a more distinctive flavour.

Example 4g

The next set of triad shapes are based around the D# Minor chord. I have used combinations of D#m, D#m7 and D#m9 chords here to create the kind of variation that's common in R&B. These chords are interchangeable, and it is best to experiment to find out which shapes and voicings you prefer. The triads below are my favourite shapes to play with.

Example 4h

Example 4i shows some ideas around the D#m triad shapes on the middle strings.

Example 4i

And now, here are some ideas based around the triads on the top three strings.

Example 4j

Now you have learned some triad licks on each individual chord shape, it's time to combine them and put them back into the original Bmaj7 – A#7#5 – D#m chord sequence.

In a normal session, I wouldn't play so many licks (less is more!) but I've written these examples to show how many possibilities can be created by combining a simple triad shape with a lick.

Example 4k

Example 4l shows another way to blend the triads with licks over the full chord sequence.

Example 4l

Lead Parts

Next, I've written a solo to help you understand how to use the decorated triad concept in a more musical way. I've broken it down into bite-sized chunks for ease of learning.

When composing the solo, I paid attention to the notes contained in the three chords: Bmaj7, A#7#5 and D#m7. They are:

Bmaj7 (B D# F# A#)

A#7#5 (A# D F#)

D#m7 (D# F# A# C#)

The first thing you may notice is that two of the chords have the note D# in common, but the A#7#5 contains a D. Knowing this led me to target that D note when the sequence moved to A#7#5, as it helped to *articulate* the chord change.

This simple idea is an incredibly useful tactic when writing a new solo. Write out the notes of each chord, then see how you can incorporate any obvious changes into your licks.

Example 4m

Sometimes it's nice to throw in a lick that's a bit flashier. The first twelve notes of this idea are based around the D# Natural Minor scale before B Major and C# Major arpeggios finish the phrase.

Example 4n

It's possible to play a diminished arpeggio starting on the major 3rd interval of a dominant chord. I've done that here to create tension over the A#7#5 chord.

Example 4o

Time for a final bit of flashiness with a lick that blends contemporary R&B/Neo-Soul with hints of Jimi Hendrix and Stevie Ray Vaughan. This lick uses the Eb Natural Minor scale, and the first half of bar one is based around an Eb Minor arpeggio to enhance the jazzy sound.

Bar two has a distinctly Hendrixy flavour and uses a variety of Eb Minor Pentatonic double-stops in the style of *The Wind Cries Mary*.

Example 4p

Now that you've learned the individual parts, it's time to put them together to play the full solo. You can watch a video of me playing the track and see how I approach each part here:

https://geni.us/acou

Example 4q

As part of your practice routine, create a chord sequence then build rhythm parts and lead parts. Use these to create a full solo with triads and pentatonic scales. If you make this a regular part of your practice time, you will quickly develop your R&B skills.

Chapter Five – Kerry "2 Smooth" Marshall

It's a pleasure to feature a track by Kerry "2 Smooth" Marshall in this book. Kerry has worked with artists like Jason Derulo, Tori Kelly, Ledisi, Sean Kingston and many others, and is among the finest R&B session guitarists in the world.

Here, he has written an R&B acoustic groove in his signature style. Here is the link to the full video. Be sure to check it out before you work through the examples below. **https://geni.us/acou**

Before we look in detail at Kerry's track, let's examine some of the ideas that crop up in his playing.

Technique Focus: Breaking Barre Chords

I will never forget the look of amazement on my student's face as I broke up a barre chord into two-note fragments. It was like a creative lightbulb lit up in his brain. Since then, it's been one of my favourite things to teach.

Let's look at how we can break a Gm7 barre chord into two-note mini chords. These shapes are foundational to R&B guitar playing so commit them to memory before moving on.

Example 5a

Next, let's split the Gm7 into three-note shapes. Some of these break the mould of traditional triad shapes, but they are equally useful.

Example 5b

The next logical step is to break the Gm7 chord voicing into four-note voicings. Although less common than two- and three-note shapes, these teach you to see barre chords as containing many textures and mini shapes within them.

Example 5c

One Kerry "2 Smooth" trademark is to take a barre chord and add colour notes that subtly change its mood.

Bars two and three in the example below show some of the tasty note choices you can add to a Gm7 shape. The specific intervals are written above the chord.

Example 5d

Here is one way to add some of these intervals into a phrase over Gm7. Those of you familiar with modern R&B guitar will have heard these ideas before in different tracks.

Example 5e

The next example shows some common additions to a GMaj7 chord. Once again, the intervals are written above the notes.

Example 5f

Example 5g is one of my favourite examples in this book. When I started to experiment by adding decorations to my barre chords, I felt a whole new level of freedom in my rhythm playing and it helped me to break away from predictable strumming and picking patterns.

Listen to the audio track before playing the example so you can hear the nuance of the phrasing.

Example 5g

Now let's look at some popular notes used to embellish a G7 chord in modern R&B.

Example 5h

Modern R&B tracks often lean heavily on rhythmic funk ideas, so here's a super funky G7 groove that uses some of the intervals in the previous example.

Example 5i

I always make sure my students can play patterns and ideas in at least two positions on the guitar. Shifting to a higher octave can really lift a track, or simply help the guitar to cut through the rest of the rhythm section.

The next set of examples shows Gm7, G7, and GMaj7 shapes with a root on the A string, and the useful note additions.

This Gm7 shape is a rhythm guitar staple and is famously used in the intro to the Doobie Brothers' *Long Train Running*.

Example 5j

Here are some classic R&B adaptions to the Gm7 chord. You may find using your 4th finger a bit of a challenge at first, but the benefits are well worth the effort.

Example 5k

Now let's look at some useful additions to the GMaj7 chord shape.

Example 5l

I first heard these GMaj7 alterations when listening to the playing of Mark Lettieri and Chris Payton. Binge-listen to their R&B work for more inspiration.

Example 5m

Here are some colourful additions to a high G7 chord shape.

Example 5n

The three-note dominant 7 chord fragment is a classic texture which can be heard in many different genres. Sliding into the chord creates a modern gospel twist. Practice sliding from different distances (from below or above) to give create nuances.

Example 5o

Acoustic Landscape – Breakdown Licks

Now let's look at the Kerry "2 Smooth" track. Example 5v shows the full solo, but first let's examine some specific ideas he uses, where every chord shape is given his signature touch.

Example 5p shows a popular R&B hammer-on/pull-off pattern on a Gm7 chord.

Example 5p

The fifth string Maj7 shape is a staple voicing of modern R&B. Here, Kerry adds hammer-ons and pull-offs on the B string to create a legato phrase.

Example 5q

The next useful shape to learn is this Dm7 voicing. Once again, Kerry decorates it by adding a fill on the B string which creates continuity with the Maj7 idea in the previous example.

Example 5r

Diminished chords play a vital role in modern R&B music and the four-string voicings shown here are especially popular. Sliding between diminished shapes is an important technique to add to your chordal repertoire.

Example 5s

This B string hammer-on and pull-off creates a sus4 sound on a major barre chord.

Example 5t

Kerry often adds a diminished chord shape on the top four strings as a passing chord. In Example 5u, he introduces an F# diminished chord between Dm7 and C.

Example 5u

With those techniques in mind, now here is the full G Minor groove that Kerry has named *Acoustic Landscape*, played at 66bpm. Don't forget to check out the video before playing through the track.

Example 5v

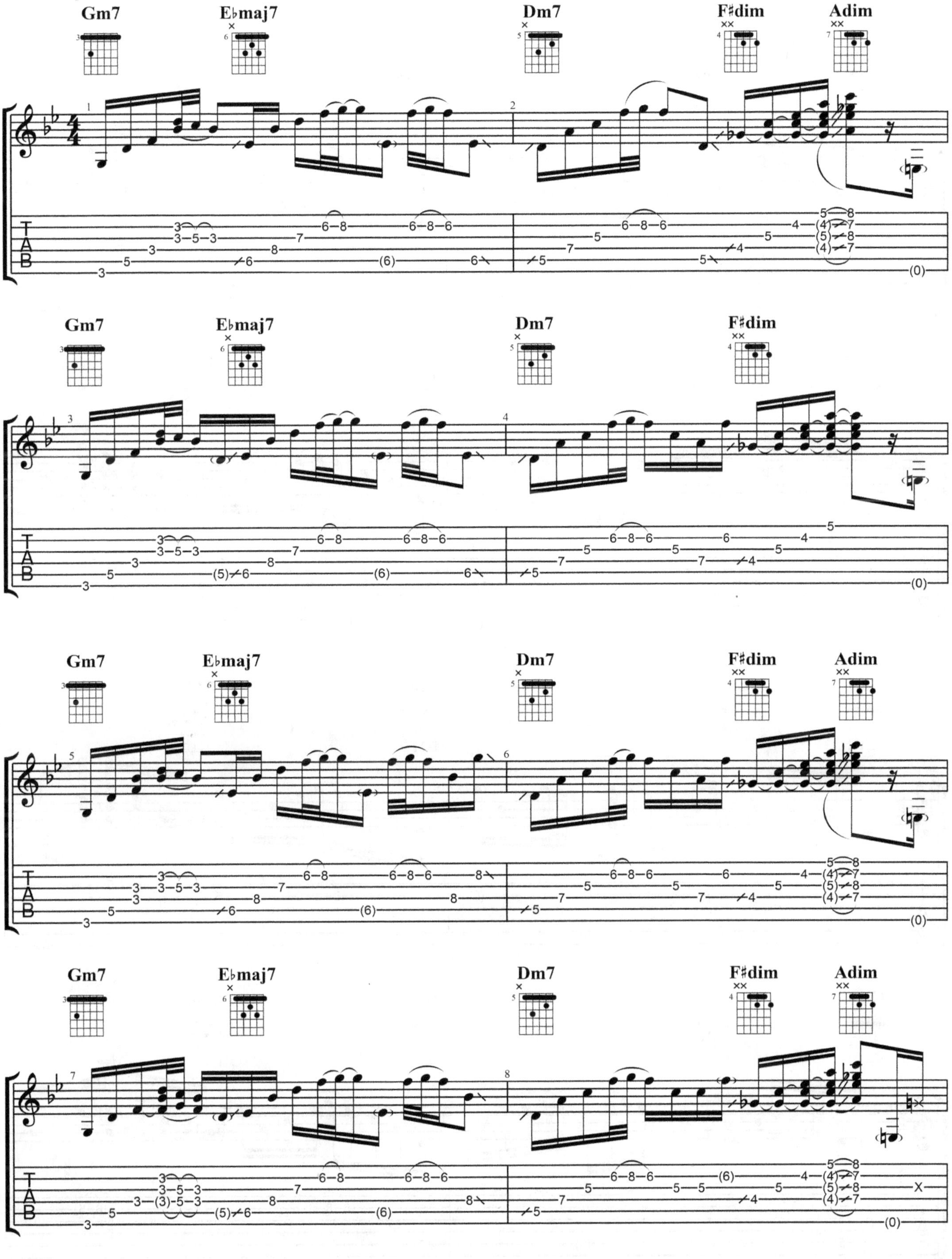
Gm7
E♭maj7
Dm7
F♯dim
Adim
Gm7
E♭maj7
Dm7
F♯dim
Gm7
E♭maj7
Dm7
F♯dim
Adim
Gm7
E♭maj7
Dm7
F♯dim
Adim

Gm7
E♭maj7
Dm7
F♯dim
Gm7
E♭maj7
Dm7
F♯dim
Adim
Gm7
E♭maj7
Dm7
F♯dim
Gm7
E♭maj7
Dm7
F♯dim
C

To discover more of Kerry's work visit **www.kerry2smooth.com**

Chapter Six – Playing Solo

So far, we've looked at a range of ideas for modern R&B guitar parts that will serve you well in a band setting. Now we turn our focus to ideas you can play on your own, without other musicians. To study these ideas, I've written two performance pieces.

We'll dissect the first tune, *Acousticy Taylor*, breaking it down into bite-sized chunks that will help you to understand my approach. Then you can try the second track, *Baching up the Wrong Tree*.

I've made performance videos of each track, so you can see and hear how I play them. **https://geni.us/acou**

Acousticy Taylor

We will begin with the main melody to my track *Acousticy Taylor*, in the key of A Major.

The foundation of this track is a chord loop of A – F#m11 – Eadd9 – DMaj7, which is interspersed with four typical R&B licks. Learn the licks separately before adding them to the full arrangement. Watch the full video before working through the following examples.

Example 6a

Example 6b uses double-stopped 6ths on non-adjacent strings. Check out the introduction to John Mayer's *Stop This Train* for a wonderful acoustic use of this approach.

Example 6b

Example 6c begins with some more beautiful 6ths based around the E Major chord. The fill on the F#m11 chord is a common R&B minor pentatonic idea.

Example 6c

This three-note D6 voicing is a useful shape for modern R&B. It's followed by a slippery legato run which uses back-to-back slides on the top two strings. Learn these slowly and make sure each slide is accurate.

Example 6d

The chordal side of R&B is one of the major reasons I started to explore the genre and Example 6e shows the kind of sequence that first hooked me. It's a classic R&B chord pattern that I've used to break up the track. Keep a guitar journal the chord voicings and patterns that most appeal to you and use them to write your own tracks.

Example 6e

The outro includes a lovely chordal run using voicings from the key of A Major. The final bar uses *slap tap* harmonics on the DMaj7 chord. To perform these, simply tap the fret wire twelve frets above the fretted note to make the harmonic sound. Watch the video to see how I perform them.

Example 6f

Acousticy Taylor had one of the best responses to any track I've released. Someone has even made it their alarm tone! It's always useful to keep party pieces like this under your belt, so you always have something to play when there isn't a vocalist around.

Example 6g

Baching up the Wrong Tree

I love to blend musical approaches to create sub-genres, and to create *Baching up the Wrong Tree* I explored what would happen if J.S. Bach wrote an acoustic R&B tune! I've included this track for two reasons. First, to teach you a fun party piece, and second to open your mind to the concept of combining genres to create your own music.

This piece is in the key of F# Minor and the licks and fills are mainly written using the F# Natural Minor scale. It's played with a capo at the 2nd fret.

Try to make each phrase sound as smooth as possible, particularly the notes that flow into a chord change. Learn this piece at around 60bpm before raising the speed in increments of 10bpm to reach the recorded tempo of 120bpm.

Example 6h

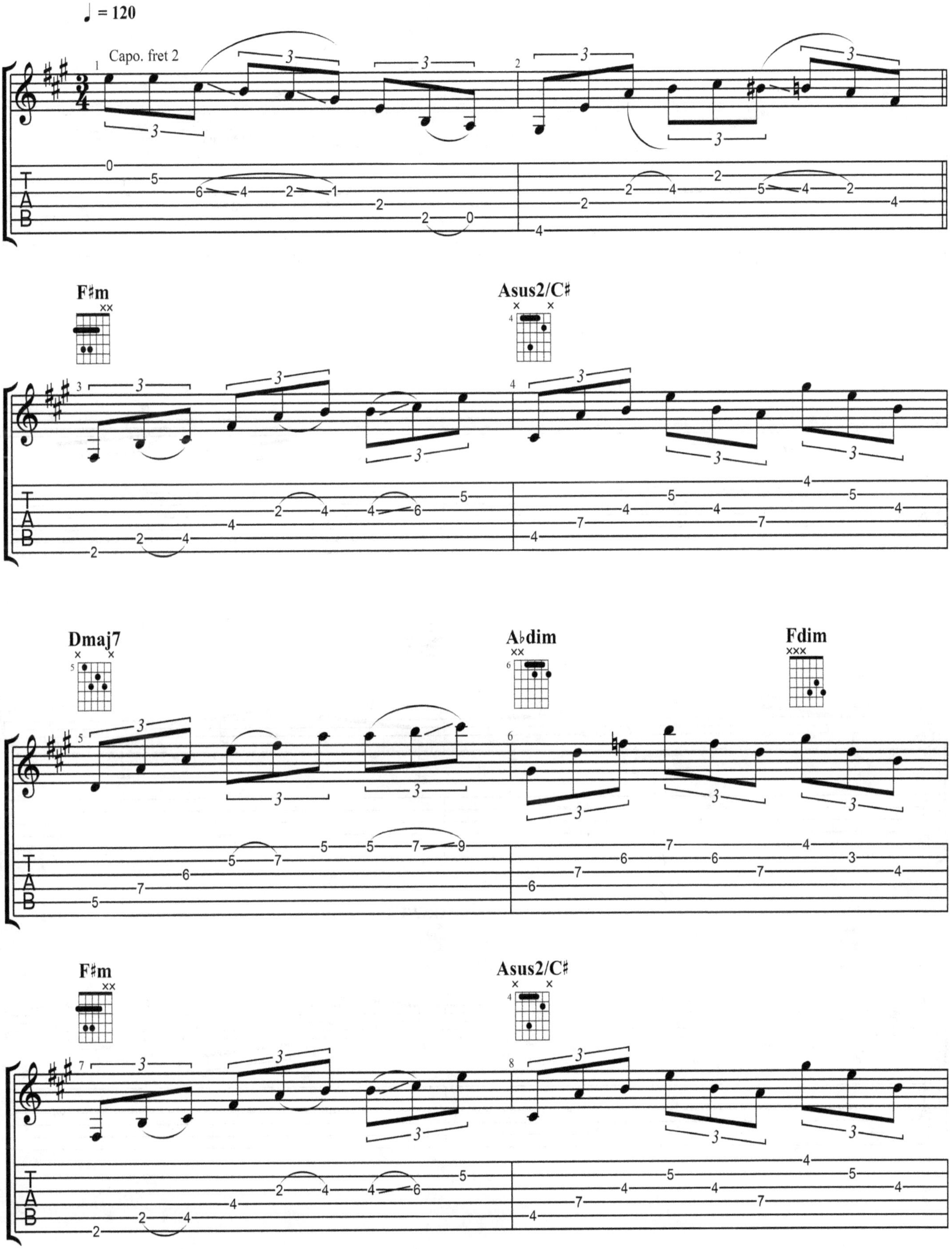
♩ = 120
Capo. fret 2
F♯m
Asus2/C♯
Dmaj7
A♭dim
Fdim
F♯m
Asus2/C♯

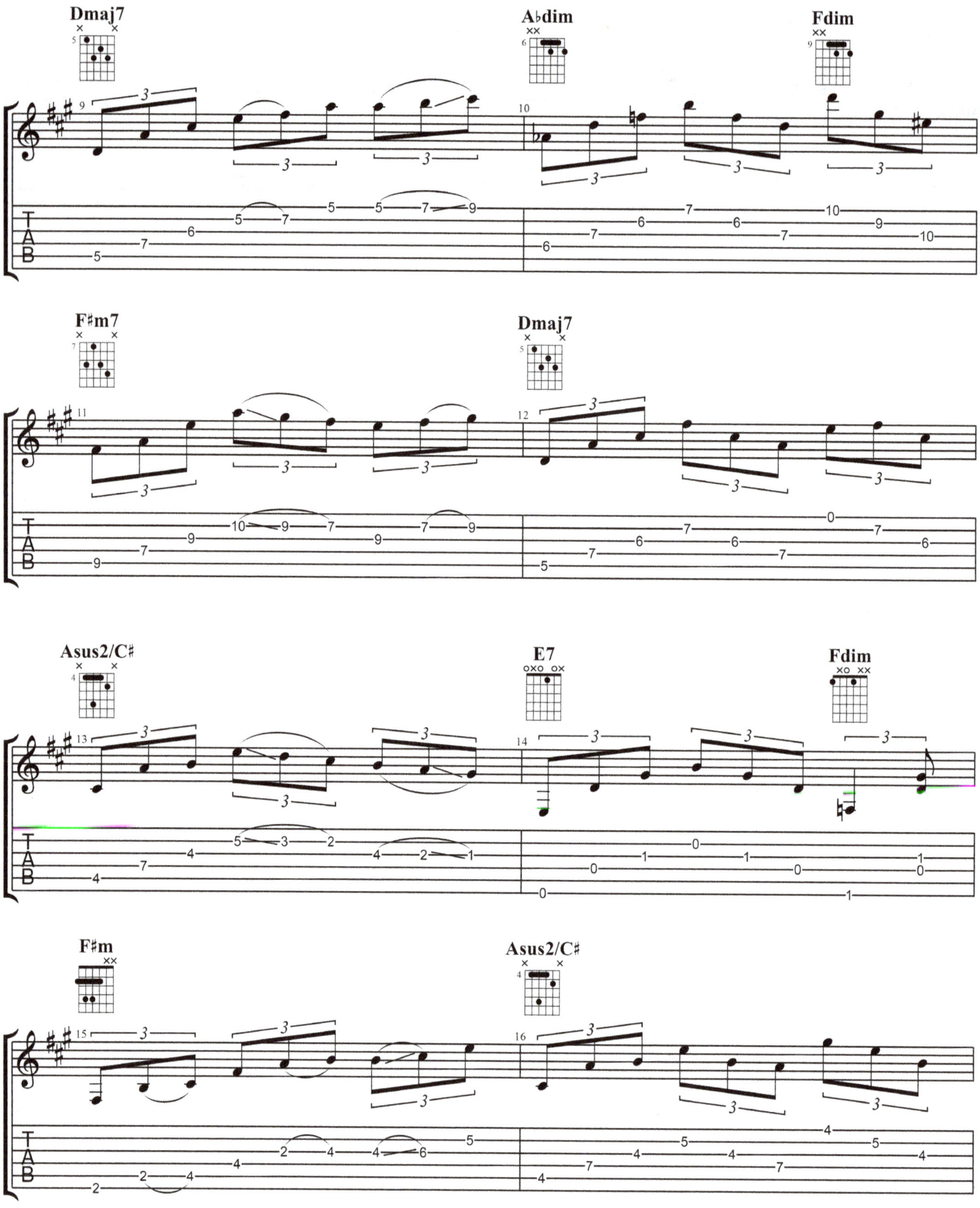
Dmaj7
A♭dim
Fdim
F♯m7
Dmaj7
Asus2/C♯
E7
Fdim
F♯m
Asus2/C♯

Now, go and can write some ideas of your own, using phrases and ideas from these two pieces. Pick and steal phrases, chord sequences and melodies that inspire you. Your R&B piece could be anywhere from a bar long to a full tune, but set yourself the goal of writing something every day.

A great starting point is the website www.splice.com where you can purchase samples that can become inspirational building blocks to create backing tracks for jamming out ideas.

Chapter Seven – Rhythmic Awareness

From the sound of a mother's heartbeat to a crowd chanting at a sports game, rhythm is the continual backdrop to our lives.

As musicians, we think of repeated rhythms as grooves, but sadly *groove* is not a well-taught or properly practiced part of guitar playing. My aim in this chapter is to teach you that groove is the core foundation of everything you play on guitar.

This time, we will build an acoustic R&B track by focusing solely on rhythm and groove. You'll learn many small, rhythm-based examples of chords and fills, then combine them to build a groove, layer by layer.

Using a metronome

Begin by learning each example with a metronome set to 50bpm and make sure every note is clean and audible. Pay attention to your picking hand to make sure you're playing the strict "down-up" alternate picking patterns written.

When you can play an example perfectly three times in a row at 50bpm, raise the speed to 53bpm and continue this way to a target speed of 80bpm or higher. This type of structured practice means you only increase your speed once the lick is played accurately.

The first example teaches you a simple E Major bassline that will be the foundation for the examples that follow.

Example 7a

Example 7b adds a rhythm to this bassline to create a funky feel. Tap your foot when you play it, to help feel the groove and stay in time.

Listen to the audio, but learn to *count* the rhythm too. I have included the counting above the notation.

Example 7b

Now let's learn a syncopated rhythm on the chords of EMaj7 and C#m7. This will form part of the groove later.

Example 7c

The four-chord loop of EMaj7 – C#m7 – F#m7 – B7 is a building block of our track. The three-note B7 voicing is a common shape in modern R&B, so memorize it before moving on.

Example 7d

Now I add a three-note passing B7 chord between EMaj7 and C#m7 to introduce some rhythmic and harmonic interest.

Example 7e

R&B rhythm guitar parts are often split between lush barre chords and single note funky lines.

Example 7f shows an example of a single note E Major Pentatonic idea that works around the chord sequence.

Example 7f

Now I add an E Major Pentatonic fill between the EMaj7 and C#m7 chords. Again, check out Hendrix's *The Wind Cries Mary* for a vast array of these double-stop ideas.

Example 7g

This E Major phrase uses double-stops on the high strings to add interest in a higher register. You can build a groove using chords, double-stops or single notes, so consider how these different textures affect the feel of a track when writing your parts. Switching between them is a great way to highlight different sections of a tune.

Example 7h

This example highlights a ringing E Major single note line that could work well as a pre-chorus or bridge section. Again, it's a simple part but it's all about the groove.

Example 7i

This idea combines a single note E Major line with a hammer-on pattern based around a C#m7 chord. Barring the C#m7 and hammering on the fourth finger takes some practice to make it sound clean but it's worth the effort.

Example 7j

Double-stops are a texture that sits between single notes and chords. This example uses E Major double-stop fragments between the 9th and 12th frets. Barre the G and B strings at the 9th fret as you perform the pull-offs.

Example 7k

This idea decorates the C#m7 chord with single notes and double-stops.

Example 7l

It's common to palm mute double-stop licks to introduce percussive textures into an R&B guitar part. Place your fretting hand close to the bridge and lightly touch the strings with the heel of your hand. The action somewhat resembles a karate chop.

Example 7m

Adding slides to double-stop licks is another way to spice them up. I first started to apply this technique to my own playing after listening to Jack Johnson's *Better Together*.

Example 7n

R&B guitar parts borrow ideas from jazz, and jazzy chord voicings are a common addition. This example introduces an F#m9 chord and a B7#5 which resolves to a more familiar EMaj7 shape. Take time to commit these chords to memory before continuing.

Example 7o

Now you've learned various different approaches to using rhythmic textures to create groove, Example 7p combines them into a single track. It uses full barre chords, double-stops and single note lines to form an R&B track in the style of Bill Withers and Isaiah Sharkey.

Example 7p

Emaj7
C♯m7
P.M.
F♯m9
A/B
B7(♯5)
Emaj7
C♯m7
let ring
F♯m7
B
B7♯5♯9
B7♯5♭9
Emaj7

Chapter Eight – *Arctic Swirl*

It's important to know that every key has its own distinctive mood or quality. I often find that moving a melody or chord sequence to a new key can completely change the feel of the track.

Arctic Swirl is a piece I wrote led by this thinking. I have always felt C# Minor to be an emotive key and the melody seemed to sit perfectly for me here.

Once again, I've broken down the key elements and techniques of this track, and we combine them at the end of the chapter.

We'll begin with the chords that form the A section of the tune: C#m7 – C#m9 – A – Eadd9 – B/D#. If any of these voicings are unfamiliar to you, take some time to learn them properly before continuing.

Example 8a

A useful technique is to play higher chord voicings with a root note on the D string. These are particularly effective at cutting through a full band mix as they allow space for other instruments to sit below them sonically.

Example 8b

The main melody of *Arctic Swirl* uses the C# Natural Minor scale and is interspersed by the chords of C#m7, A Major, Eadd9 and B/D#. It's my favourite bit of writing in the book and forms part of my daily practice.

Learn the melody line and chords separately before piecing them together.

Example 8c

Example 8d shows the second part of the A section. The C#m9 in bar one incorporates the open B and E strings and allows them to ring Try this idea in your own arrangements.

As with the previous example, learn the melody line and chords separately before putting them together.

Example 8d

The B section of *Arctic Swirl* opens with the chord sequence A – B – Cdim7 – C#m7. The fourth bar teaches you one of my favourite blues phrases.

Example 8e

The outro is based around C# Minor Pentatonic double-stops. Bar two is one of the most important phrases in R&B/Neo-Soul guitar playing and is often used in introductions and outros.

Example 8f

Now let's combine these parts into the full track. Check out the video of me performing the track at **https://geni.us/acou**

Example 8g

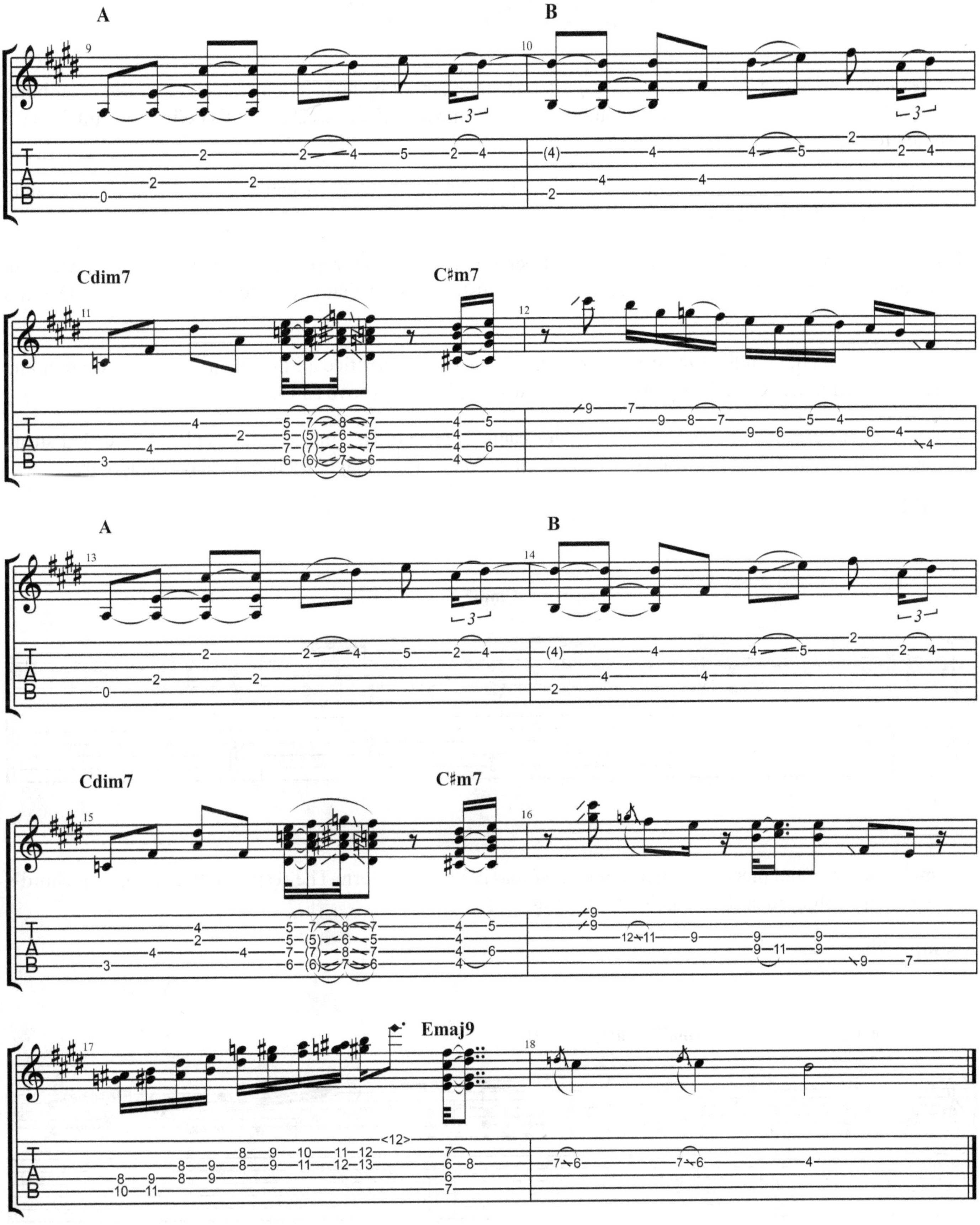
A
B
Cdim7
C♯m7
A
B
Cdim7
C♯m7
Emaj9

Chapter Nine – *Dual Bliss*

Now for a piece that can be played as a two-guitar arrangement or by using a loop pedal. *Dual Bliss* combines a steady R&B vamp and a chordal riff, before launching into a stylistic R&B solo. It's definitely a track that's designed to impress!

In the video you'll see that I use a pick to play the solo, but the other parts can be played fingerstyle or with hybrid picking. Check it out: **https://geni.us/acou**

This piece is played with a capo at the 3rd fret. I personally use Kyser capos, although any decent brand will do. If you don't have a capo, you can play it without, just remember that you'll be out of tune with the audio tracks.

I have included an 82bpm R&B/Neo Soul drum track so you can practice all the examples in this chapter and not just the final piece. Create your own examples using this cool groove as well.

Let's begin with the main theme of the piece. For each of the chords, a melody line is played with a G string hammer-on and you'll need to barre your first finger on each of the Maj7 voicings to play it smoothly.

Example 9a

The main theme of the piece is built around a *call and response* pattern. The response to the opening chord's call riff is an E Blues idea shown in bar two below.

Example 9b

These Em7 fragments are built on the middle strings and often used in guitar quartet and R&B gospel settings. Bar two introduces some lovely voicings of CMaj6, B7#5, and a Bsus4 that resolves to E Minor later in the track.

Example 9c

The B7(11) and Em11 chords are useful voicings that live on the jazzier side of R&B. The run-down of E Minor chord shapes in bar two is also a common R&B device. Try transposing this example to all keys for a great chordal workout!

Example 9d

Next is the main melody, written using the E Natural Minor and E Harmonic Minor scales. I keep the melody on the higher strings, so it cuts through above the chords.

The lick that begins at the end of bar three is an E Blues scale idea with some added chromaticism. It contains two rhythmic groupings of sextuplets, and to play these accurately I say a six-syllable word, such as re-spon-si-bi-li-ty to keep the triplets in time. Listen to the audio track to hear how I phrase this example.

Example 9e

The first six notes of Example 8f are based around one of the most famous jazz licks ever played, built from a chromatic idea around an E Minor arpeggio. If you want to add some jazzy sophistication to your playing, this line is a great start!

Example 9f

When I first heard *Velours* by Anomalie Beats, I was blown away. Although it is played on keyboard, I figured out a way to play it on guitar. It was difficult, but it taught me how to create these modern R&B/ Neo-Soul double-stop patterns.

Here, I pay a small homage to that track by using chromatic double-stops in E Minor. Although playing this example with downstrokes is easier at first, learning it with alternate picking is worth the effort, especially when you want to play it at a higher speed.

Go and listen to the live version of *Velours* on YouTube – it's fantastic!

Example 9g

Now you have all the building blocks of the tune, it's time to put it all together.

There's no backing track for *Dual Bliss* as I want to encourage you to jam with another guitarist (or with yourself using a looper pedal or recording software). It's great fun!

The first four bars written below should be looped (or played by another musician).

Example 9h

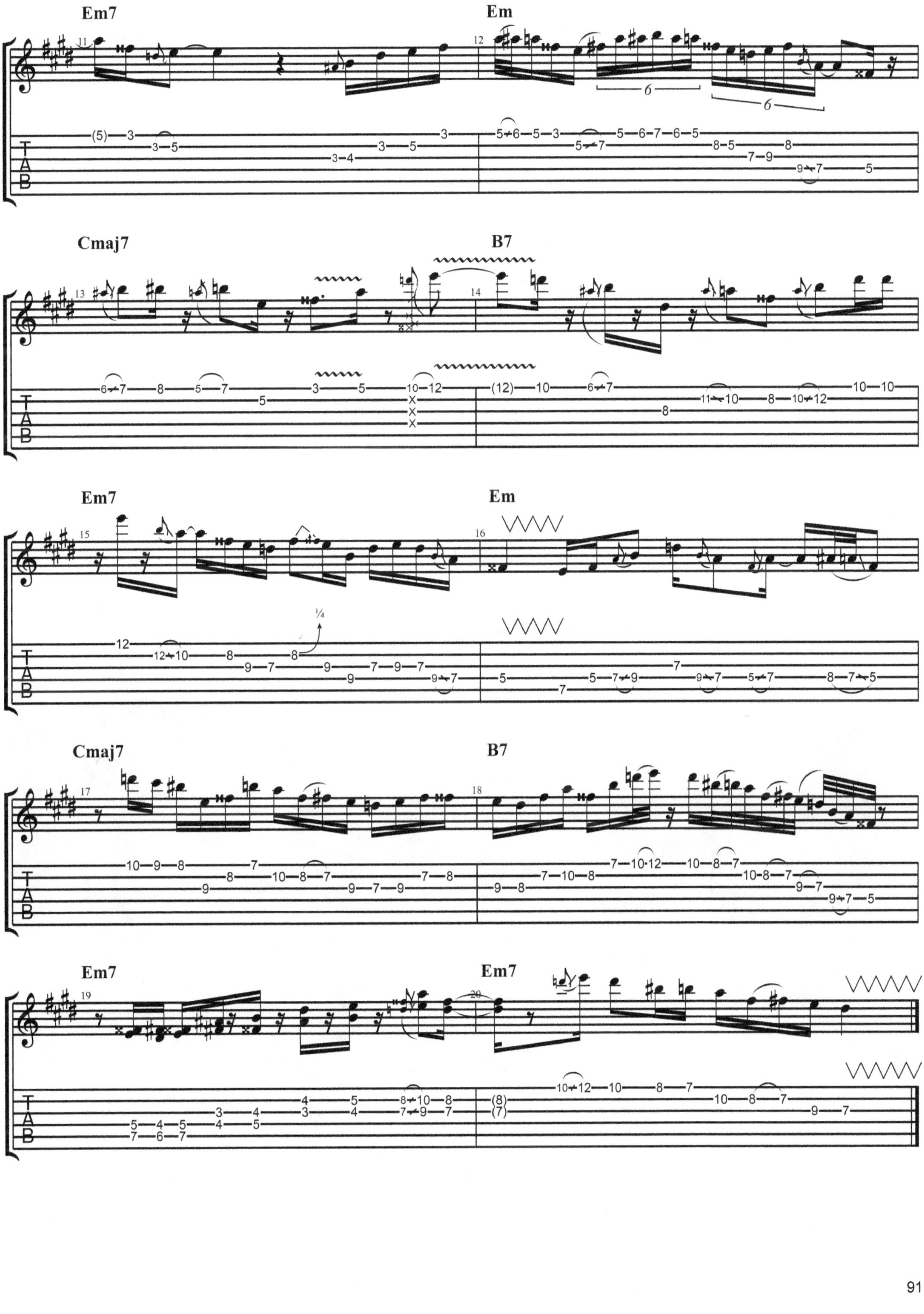
Em7
Em
Cmaj7
B7
Em7
Em
Cmaj7
B7
Em7
Em7

Playing with a guitarist who is a similar level to you can be a great blessing as you progress on your musical journey. Going to local jam nights or reaching out on the Fundamental Changes Facebook forum are potential starting points to find some new people to make music with.

Chapter Ten – *Giraffe in a Scarf*

My track, *Penguin Suit* is one of the most popular things I've ever written and it went somewhat viral after I included it **The NeoSoul Guitar Book**, a Fundamental Changes bestseller I co-wrote with Kristof Neyens. *Giraffe in a Scarf* is my follow up track and I hope it's as popular!

It also gave me the opportunity to buy a 4-foot giraffe to feature in the video, much to the bemusement of the mail man! Check out the video here: **https://geni.us/acou**

Giraffe in a Scarf is in the key of A Minor and written around the A Natural Minor scale. I mainly use hybrid picking, but by all means experiment with using your fingers or a pick to see which you prefer. It's fun to take a different approach on each sections of the song.

Let's break down some of the core themes of this piece into individual exercises.

We will begin with the A Blues introduction lick – a double-stop idea played on the top three strings. Learn the first four notes and repeat them until they feel comfortable. Then, learn the next set of four before combining the two parts.

Example 10a

The double-stop lick in bar one is built around A Harmonic Minor, but the phrase in bar two is a legato A Blues idea. Blending different types of minor scales is a common technique and a useful writing tool to consider when composing.

Example 10b

Example 10c introduces the main theme of the piece. It is actually one of my favourite things to play in this book as it combines single note fills and three-note gospel voicings with a percussive feel. Learn the chord shapes first and commit them to memory before tackling the single note lines.

This type of chordal approach is popular in quartet guitar playing and you should check out the music of Chris Payton to hear some excellent ideas in this genre.

Example 10c

The B section revolves around the chords FMaj7, E7 and Am7, and I find it a great way to warm up my grooves, chords, and fills all at once. In fact, if you had to pick four bars from this entire book to impress your friends, then I suggest you choose these!

Example 10d

The C section is based around similar chords to the B section but adds a Dm7 to E7 turnaround. Another difference is that the FMaj7 and E7 chords are played using much lower voicings.

Example 10e

I learnt this Am11 voicing from a Kerry "2 Smooth" Instagram video. I loved the sound of the ringing notes performed by the pull-offs to open strings. I often try adding pull-offs to open strings to see what new tonalites I can create. Some sound fantastic and some sound terrible. Try to only play the fantastic ones!

Example 10f

This legato lick crams as many notes in as possible before resolving to the Am9 chord in bar two. While this lick is obviously written for speed, take your time and make sure you can play each hammer-on and slide cleanly at a slower tempo before speeding up.

Example 10g

So here we are – you're ready to play *Giraffe in a Scarf*!

I wanted to end this book with a bang, not just by combining all my favourite licks and ideas in one tune, but by also recording a video to make you smile. If you have worked through this chapter and learned the licks individually, you will be well prepared to tackle this tune, which is played at 90bpm.

Example 10h

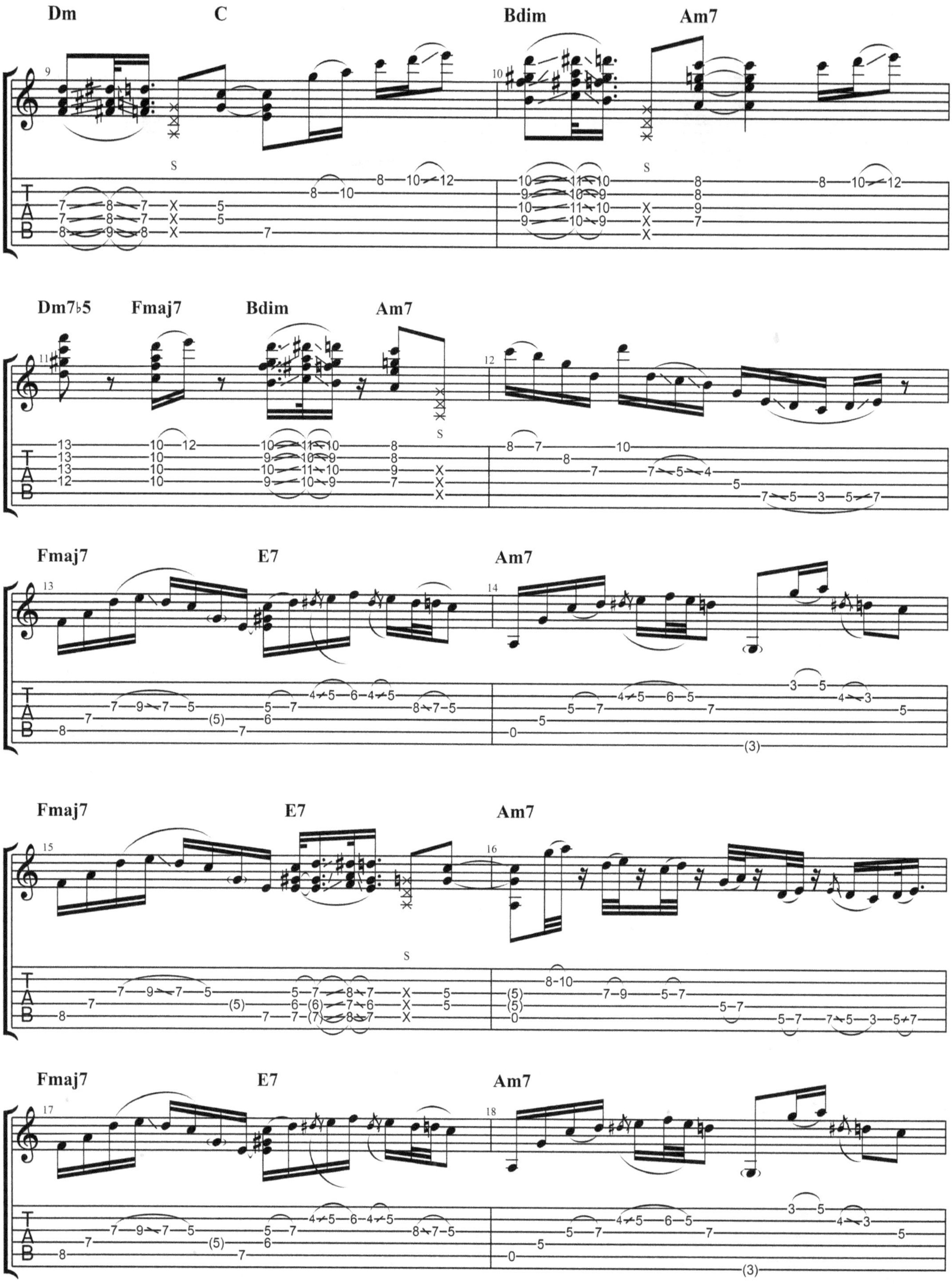
Dm
C
Bdim
Am7
Dm7♭5
Fmaj7
Bdim
Am7
Fmaj7
E7
Am7
Fmaj7
E7
Am7
Fmaj7
E7
Am7

Fmaj7 E7 Am7
S
Fmaj7 E7 Am7 Dm7 E7
Fmaj7 E7 Am7 G/B C E7
Fmaj7 E7 Am7 Dm7 E7
Fmaj7 E7 A♭dim(♯5) Am11

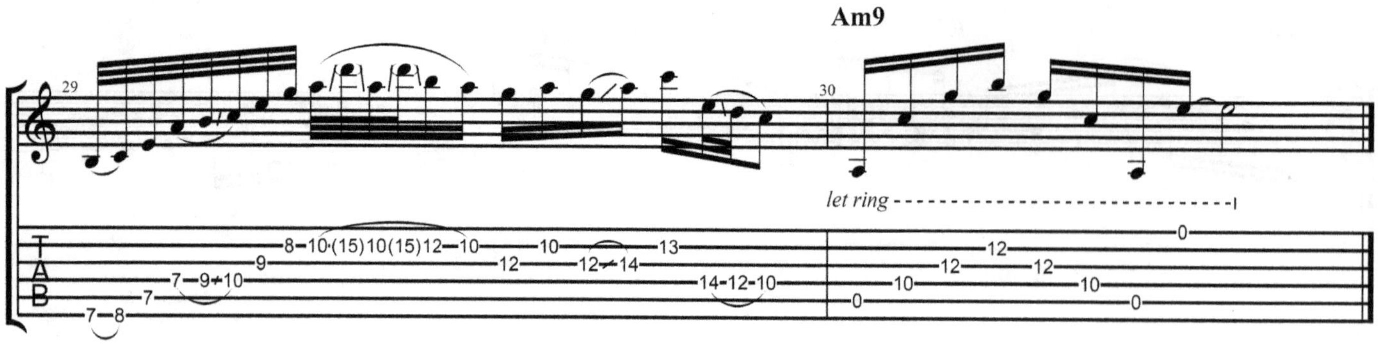
Am9
29
30
let ring
T
A
B

Conclusion

Well done! You made it!

I've crammed a huge number of ideas into this book and my hope is that it will be a valuable resource for you for many years to come.

I want you to use my examples as a starting point for creating your own modern R&B patterns, phrases and songs. Let your ears guide you and don't rely on just reaching for the "safe" notes – you should always be looking to explore. Remember the saying, "If it sounds good, it is. If it sounds bad, it probably is too", but don't be afraid to make mistakes while reaching for new ideas.

An important musical goal is to play with other people, so while you are developing your skills, find time to jam with other musicians. Playing with other instrumentalists is literally the best way to improve your musicianship.

My passion in life is teaching people to express themselves through guitar, so if you have any questions, please get in touch and I'll do my best to respond as quickly as possible.

You can contact me at simeypratt@gmail.com or via **www.fundamental-changes.com**

You can also check out my Instagram Channel to see what I am up to in my own playing.

@simeygoesfunkay

By the Same Author

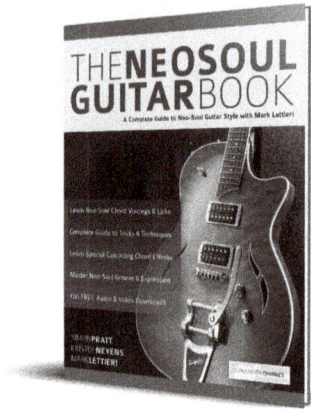

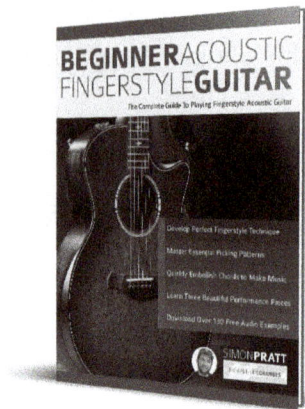

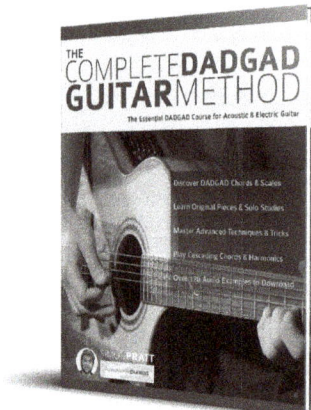

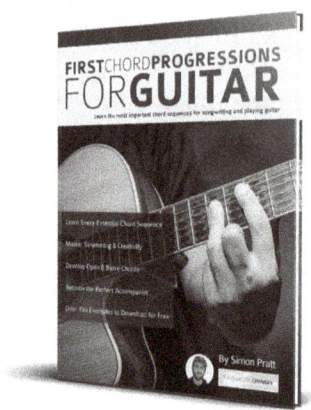

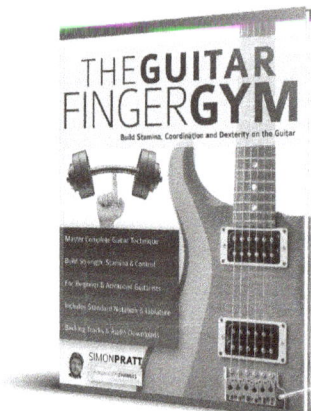

www.ingramcontent.com/pod-product-compliance
Lightning Source LLC
Chambersburg PA
CBHW081432090426
42740CB00017B/3273